Moshup's Footsteps

The Wampanoag Nation
Gay Head/Aquinnah

The People of First Light

Helen Vanderhoop Manning

HELEN MANNING

with

Jo-Ann Eccher

Blue Cloud Across the Moon Publishing Company
Aquinnah, MA

Moshup's Footsteps

The Wampanoag Nation
Gay Head/Aquinnah

The People of First Light

by

Helen Manning

with

Jo-Ann Eccher

Blue Cloud Across the Moon Publishing Company
Aquinnah, Massachusetts 02535

Copyright © 2001
by Helen Manning
All rights reserved.

Library of Congress Card Number: 00-192987
ISBN 0-9706686-0-0

Dedication

To the Wampanoags of Aquinnah—the people of the first light—who have kept the legends alive. And, to my friend Shelagh Ui Neill-Nitze, who insisted we finish this story.

Thanks for the valuable research assistance and friendship of Jo-Ann Eccher. Thanks to Tobias Vanderhoop and the Wampanoag Language Revitalization Project; and, to Jessie Little Doe Fermina for her love of the language. Special thanks to the memories held by those who contributed to this book and have passed over: Helen Attaquin, Alfred Vanderhoop, Ada Manning, Maysel Vanderhoop, Thelma Weissberg, Ida Colby and Winona Silva. And, thanks to Bertha Robinson for sharing her memories. Photographs are from the family collection of Helen Manning as well as courtesy of the Martha's Vineyard Historical Society Archives. This book is supported, in part, by a grant from the Aquinnah Cultural Council, Chilmark Cultural Council, Edgartown Cultural Council, the Oak Bluffs Cultural Council, the Tisbury Cultural Council, and the West Tisbury Cultural Council—local cultural agencies that are supported by the Massachusetts Cultural Council, a state agency.

Tremendous gratitude to Barbara Perrin for her assistance with graphic design and production.

Aquinnah

The Wampanoags of Gay Head/Aquinnah have lived continuously, for centuries, at Aquinnah, a 3400 acre peninsula, situated at the southwestern tip of the island of Noepe—the land surrounded by bitter waters—or Martha's Vineyard. The common translation for the Wampanoag word Aquinnah is "land under the hill" or "land at the end of the shore". There are 480 acres of Tribal Trust Lands which include the Common Lands of the Cranberry Bogs on Lobsterville, the Herring Creek, and the Gay Head Cliffs. Other lands owned by the tribe include parcels in Christiantown and Chappaquidick and other small lots in Aquinnah.

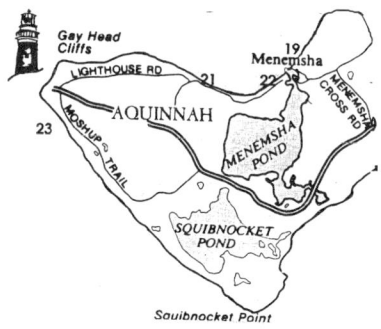

Town of Aquinnah

Population Year round: 308   Seasonal population: 1450
Wampanoag Population: There are 966 tribal members with 350 members living on island. One hundred and fifty Wampanoags live in Aquinnah.

Noepe's Eastern Algonquin Names

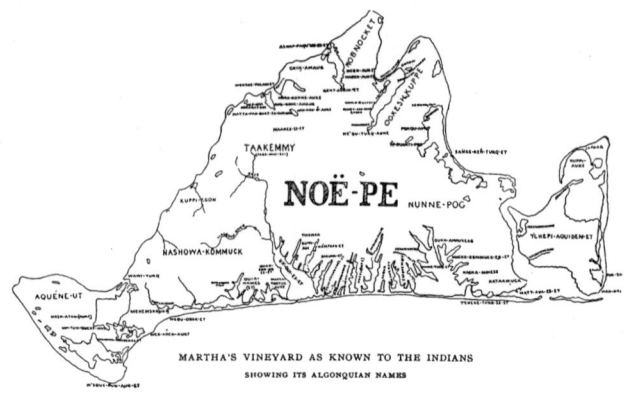

Banks, History of Martha's Vineyard, Vol 1, Dukes County Historical Society 1966

The Original Four Sachemships

Taakemmy: *place to grind corn* (West Tisbury)
Nunne-pog: *when there is water there* (Edgartown)
Tchepiaquidenet: *the separate island* (Chappaquidick)
Aquinnah: *land under the hill or end of the shoreline* (Aquinnah)

Other Place Names

Nobnocket: *dry place* (Vineyard Haven/Tisbury)
Nashowa-Kommock: *place in the middle* (Chilmark)
Sengekontacket: *place where the brook flows into the river* (Oak Bluffs)
Tashmoo: *pure water, great spring*
Katama: *crab fishing place*
Menemshaunk-Menemsha: *place for whale*s

For more information on Wampanoag places on Noepe see the Wampanoag Way Map available at the Wampanoag Tribal Building, Aquinnah, MA.

*Beulah Salisbury Vanderhoop (1815 -1882),
my Wampanoag great grandmother,
married my great grandfather,
William Adrian Vanderhoop (1816 - 1893),
from Surinam and the Netherlands.*

When the legends die, the dreams end.
When the dreams end, there is no more greatness.

— Pawkunnawkuts People

Over and over again one hears the comment, "Gay Head is not Gay Head anymore". I imagine, now that the town's name has been changed from Gay Head back to its original Wampanoag name, Aquinnah—land under the hill—some will say Aquinnah is not Aquinnah anymore. Yet, from my perspective (a Wampanoag woman, born in Aquinnah) this special place will always exist because the Wampanoags, People of the First Light, have woven a spirit-filled fabric using the threads of history, culture and legends to honor the story of the Wampanoag Nation—past, present and future. I, and other Wampanoags living on Noepe, land surrounded by bitter waters, or as commonly called Martha's Vineyard—hold the common belief that the kind and gentle giant, Moshup, created the island, taught us how to fish and catch whales, and is a presence in our daily lives. We believe we are the children of Moshup and by holding on to our beliefs and legends we have been able to reclaim our language, gain federal tribal recognition and reacquire our Common Lands including the Cranberry Bogs, the Herring Creek and the face of the Aquinnah Cliffs.

Helen Manning, 2000

Wunee Keesug: Good Day

I cannot help but be influenced by Moshup's spirit on my daily walks on the beach. I hear foot steps, the fog rolls in; is it Ole' Moshup and his companion Squant? They tell me that they want their stories to be told. These stories come to me bundled in the sacred fog blown my way. I agree to write down their stories because even though the island has always appealed to scientists, tourists, and others who enjoy simple and natural beauty, there is little information about Aquinnah and the Wampanoags. For a long, long time now I have wanted to tell these stories. I have wanted to sit down with you and have a long conversation just like we would do years ago before everyone got so busy. This book has been written to remedy this.

Author Helen Manning at the Aquinnah Light

Memories of Aquinnah

I was born in Aquinnah on September 24, 1919. My father, Arthur Herbert Vanderhoop, is Wampanoag and my mother, Evelyn Moss, is African American, or as she would say in her day, *colored*. My father's mother was Josephine Smalley and his father was Cummings Bray Vanderhoop. His paternal grandmother was Beulah Salisbury and his grandfather was William Adrian Vanderhoop. William Adrian was of Dutch and Surinase descent and met my great grandmother here on Noepe when he was traveling up and down the Atlantic Coast on a merchant trade ship. Their meeting in the 1830s, subsequent marriage, and beautiful family of nine children began the Vanderhoops on Noepe.

Helen Manning and her parents in Aquinnah, 1920.

My home has always been near the Aquinnah Cliffs, the most sacred place on the Island. I live in a house in the shadow of the lighthouse's beacon, not far from Moshup's Den; and, just to be safe, I'd better say that I'm not far from Cheepie's mischievous ways. (Cheepie is our trickster, so I always acknowledge him or pay the consequences.)

As a child, when I looked to the east I saw six small houses and I knew every family living in each house. Now I can see over twenty houses and I still only know who lives in six of them. Growing up, if you were from Aquinnah, well, that was synonymous with being a Wampanoag. It meant that your ancestors had lived here continuously for centuries before you.

Many non-Wampanoags are not aware that before the 1600s Wampanoags, and other Native Peoples of the Eastern Algonquin Nations, were visiting and residing on the island, enjoying its rich hunting and fishing grounds, for over 10,000 years. By the year 2270 BC, we Wampanoags had made Noepe our permanent home. When the English arrived, we lived all over this island. We had inland winter encampments, protected from the fierce nor-easters, and summer villages near fertile lands and good fishing grounds. With the coming of the English in 1642, we almost lost everything including our land and language. That is how we ended up in Aquinnah, home of Moshup.

We first came to Aquinnah to escape the illness and disease that the English brought with them, to which we had no immunity. We came to Aquinnah because we were being displaced when some of our leaders, or Sachems, transfered the Sachemship to the English. The English cleared the land and put up fences and the majority of us were forced to leave. Others came to Aquinnah to escape the English missionaries' attempts to pacify us through Christianity. History has proven that we are survivors. Even though we almost lost our language, we never lost our culture. We have many languages besides our spoken language including the songs we sing, the heartbeat of the drum and our legends. We have never forgotten our legends.

When I was growing up in the 1920s, every family had chickens, a cow, a pig and vegetable garden and, most important, every family had a home. I remember eating fish, lobster, scallops, venison, chowder, cranberries, plum porridge made with milk, raisins and nutmeg, nocake (a traditional dish of parched fine-ground corn) and homemade ice cream flavored with coffee and fresh peaches. Even if you left the community to go whaling for years or to go to college, when you came home you had a place to live. Land was not at a premium like it is today.

For years Aquinnah was considered remote and inconvenient. We did not have a fine harbor. We did not have electricity and phones until the 1950s. Then there was the time in the 1970s and 1980s when we reclaimed our power and people were afraid to buy land in Aquinnah for fear they would lose it in our land claim. Of course, now it is almost an impossible dream for children born here to think they will be able to own land unless they are willing to pay a very high price. That is why the tribe fought to bring affordable housing to Aquinnah, so our children could keep the dream of Moshup alive.

My mother and father ran a hotel and restaurant, the Not-A-Way, just down from the lighthouse. For electricity we had our own system with a series of car batteries, and for water we had a cistern to collect the rain water or we carried water up from the spring. The specialty at the restaurant was quahog chowder, lobster sandwiches and lobster dinners with my mother's special mayonnaise, french fries, and apple and blueberry pies.

Gay Head Light and Not-A-Way Inn

When I turned school age, my life changed in that I began to only spend summers in Aquinnah and we went to my mother's family, in Washington, DC, during the school year. In those days when we traveled from the Vineyard, we took the boat to New Bedford, on to New York via a boat from Fall River, and then finally on to D.C. via train. It was a two day trip. When my father arrived in D.C. at the end of the season, he would be loaded with cranberries, sausages, fresh pork, hazelnuts and other bounty from Aquinnah.

When I returned each summer, one of my tasks was to be a lookout for the arrival of the order cart. About three times a week a cart carrying meat and other staples would come. Another vendor had vegetables and fruit. There also was the ice man, with blocks of ice to keep our food fresh in ice boxes since we did not have gas or electricity.

During my entire childhood, I wished that I could remain in Aquinnah. Even after attending Miner Teachers College, and working in Washington D.C., I never let go of my dream of returning. In 1956 my wish came true. I discovered the town needed a teacher for the one room school house: six grades, fifteen students. It was the same school where my mother, Evelyn Moss Vanderhoop, had taught. I qualified and it proved to be one of the best experiences of my life. I thank my creator everyday.

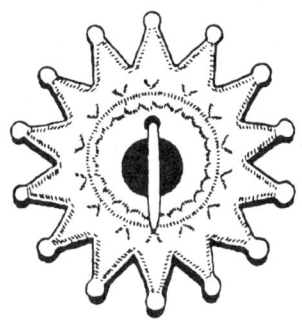

Five Hundred Years Ago

Imagine yourself 500 years ago, seated on the earthen floor of an old wigwam or *wetu*, which has been swept with a corn husk broom and sprinkled with white beach sand in honor of a gala occasion—a happening of songs and stories. As you look outside, you see only paths and trails; no roads, no telephone and electric poles, no stone walls, no fences, no houses, no lighthouse. The landscape is one great expanse of sand dunes, trees, bushes, vines, open land ready for cultivation, rounded wetus, and a ceremonial long house with smoke rising. Fields are planted with corn, beans, squash, and tobacco for ceremonies. You can hear drumming and chanting in the early morning as people pray in the sweat lodges and run into the ocean as a means of purification. You can hear the ocean, the wind, maybe children playing, and the crackling of twigs under the hoofs of an animal or the feet of a hunter. In the distance off shore you can see European explorers who have been stopping here since the year 1006 AD: Thorfinn, Champlain, Verrazzano and Gosnold. More than 500 ships come and go each year. Everyone who passes is impressed by the beauty and generosity of the inhabitants.

The women are outside weaving mats to cover the *wetus*, planting the gardens, gathering berries, tending their children, and caretaking the tobacco fields. The men are making canoes, arrow heads and bows, spears for fishing, and tools for planting. They live according to a seasonal schedule, using only what is needed.

The traditional home or wetu

The Legends of Moshup

We Wampanoags had no written language until the English arrived. Our history was kept through the telling of our legends. At night, after the chores had been completed, people would gather around the fire and listen to our elders tell our legends. This is how the legends have passed from generation to generation. Our legends are the stories that allow us to gain a better understanding of our past and explain our history to our children. The legends of my people, the Wampanoags of Aquinnah, center around Moshup. He is a benevolent being of gigantic proportions, responsible for forming the island of Martha's Vineyard and the surrounding islands. I remember my grandmother telling me that he was "taller than the tallest tree and as large around as the spread of a full grown pine". He is responsible for our knowledge of the resources of the sea and gives us coastal fog when he wants to remind us that he is still around. Moshup lived with his wife, Squant, and their many children in Moshup's Den, nestled in the colored clay cliffs of Aquinnah. It is where he watched over the people of Aquinnah, not far from where the Gay Head Light still keeps watch over travelers and fishing people.

Moshup's School

Moshup's Den was the first school in Aquinnah. Each day Moshup would gather all his children to teach them how to maintain a good life. He was the first teacher in a continuously-run school, of which I was the last teacher. When the school closed in 1968, there were five children in four grades. It was one of the last one-room schoolhouses in the United States.

When I was the teacher, the school was like a home situation. The children and I planned the day together, with older students helping the younger. We would make a big pot of soup for lunch. The natural world also served as our classroom and we would study the pond out in back, watch the birds at the birdfeeder, take walks and talk about nature and the changing of the seasons. We would also include arithmetic, spelling and art.

Gay Head School 1959-1960

Some people wanted the school to close because they said it was not competitive enough. Well, my philosophy was always about cooperation. It was the same when I first became a teacher on the Island. At my first island-wide school meeting, I mentioned that we were studying the Wampanoags and their contributions. "Oh my," said one of the teachers, "won't that interfere with you completing the social studies text?" (The text, of course, did not have a word in it about the Wampanoags.) Now, everyone wants a tribal member to come speak to their classes about the Wampanoags.

Moshup Forms the Island Noepe

Land Amidst the Bitter Waters

Ten thousand years ago Martha's Vineyard, or Noepe, was not even an island. It was an elevated portion of an extensive coastline that extended more than 70 miles out into the Atlantic Ocean. When Moshup was a child, he would accompany his father as he traveled along the eastern seaboard to hunt and fish. Moshup's father, like Moshup, was taller than the tallest tree and both could see far into the distance as they traveled through the Wampanoag Nation—which is now Rhode Island, Connecticut and Massachusetts. So, more than 5,000 years ago, Moshup got a glimpse of the coastal plain and told his father that was where he wanted to settle; there was a magical call to him. Everything was perfect there and no one was yet continuously living on the coastal plain; rather, people were coming and going to fish and hunt.

Moshup had lots of cousins and they were all named Moshup too. He gathered them together and told them of the beauty at Aquinnah and the abundance of whales and game meat for food. Moshup was not happy on the mainland. So, after long and careful consideration, he decided he would search out a new place where he and his followers might live in peace. He invited all who wanted to come to follow him to this new home.

Moshup wandered along marshes, over the dunes and through the forest. After dragging his huge foot, Moshup paused to look around and the ocean rushed to form a pool behind him. The pool deepened and became a channel; and, the waves, along with the full moon tides, formed the wide opening which now separates the Elizabeth Islands, and Cappoaquit/ Noman's Land. Still, it was the land ahead where Moshup wished to live in peace. So, he again dragged his great toes, permitting the waters of the ocean to rush in and surround the land we now know as the island of Martha's Vineyard. He dragged his foot once again and the majestic Aquinnah cliffs appeared.

The travels were long and there were difficulties such as high tides and sea monsters. His cousins and their families became tired and decided to settle on various points on the Island, setting up villages with their own forms of government known as Sachemships. These were small villages with a number of extended families, led by a council of elders. The Sachemships included Takemmy, mid-island place to grind corn; Nunne-pog, the water people; and Chappaquidick, separate island. Each Sachemship was led by a Sachem whose power was dependent on the consent of the village. Confident that his cousins had set up a system that would be free from the discord he had left on the mainland, Moshup bid farewell to his cousins and continued his journey to the Aquinnah Cliffs where he established the Sachemship of Aquinnah.

Soon after, a Pawkunnawkut (Wampanoag) Indian who lived on the mainland, near the brook which was dug out by the great trout, was caught with his dog upon one of the pieces of floating ice, and carried to Noepe. For many years,

Wampanoags assumed that Noepe was the residence of Hobbamock, the being who rules over evil, breeds storms in the air, and utters the fearful sound in the black clouds. So, when the hunter and his dog arrived here, he was surprised to meet Moshup, his wife Squant, and their children. In the spring, he returned to his camp and told his community about the wonderful Moshup who had been kind towards him as he drove the whales near the shore. The man, and his family and neighbors, decided to move to Noepe to be closer to Moshup.

Moshup, his wife Squant, and their twelve sons and twelve daughters, settled in their new home at the clay cliffs of Aquinnah, which, at that time, reached a mile out to sea. Moshup would stand on the multicolored cliffs and look out to see impending danger, as well as food to easily provide for his family and others. He always shared his bounty—a trait that continues today in Aquinnah.

Moshup was fond of whale meat and would eat a whole whale at a meal. Standing near the entrance of his den, he could reach out over the cliffs, pick up a whale that had been washed ashore, and swing it over to his continuously burning fire. The blood and grease from the whales stained the cliffs red. The charcoal from the fires gave the cliffs a band of black clay.

In 1602 the European explorer Gosnold, upon seeing the gaily colored cliffs, renamed Aquinnah "Gay Head". He put Gay Head on his maps and when he returned to England, everyone referred to the place as Gay Head. No one even considered that we already had named it. It took us almost 400 years to reclaim the name. Since the year 2000, the town is once again known as Aquinnah.

The collection of fossils found in the Aquinnah Cliffs contain New England's most complete record of the past one hundred million years of geologic history. The Aquinnah Cliffs tell the story of a land first covered with forests, then engulfed by seawater with giant sharks swimming over what are now meadows. The fossils contained in the cliffs range from the teeth of fifty feet long sharks to the fossil of the oldest flower known in the world—75 million years old. The fossils tell the story of a time when horses and camels roamed the plains of Aquinnah. Geological studies tell of the glacial flows crushing together forest, desert, and ocean and depositing the fossils over 10,000 years ago. Others say that the fossils are simply Moshup's compost pit—with all those whales and sharks he ate, surely he had to put the bones somewhere!

The Cliffs of Aquinnah

The Aquinnah Cliffs

For the Wampanoags, the Aquinnah Cliffs are a sacred site. Spirits of the past still live there and when people disrespect this area, it is very detrimental to my soul. This is why we ask you not to climb the cliffs, dig into the clay, nor cover your bodies with the clay.

The multi-colored clay from the cliffs has been used to make our traditional, non-fired, pottery and jewelry. It also has been a source of income. At one time, each tribal member could harvest 13 tons of clay. This clay was used for dishes and bricks on the mainland. Especially valuable was the white clay, known as kaolin, which was used to make dishes off-island. The clay agent would pay $3-$5 per ton for the clay (five dollars if you brought it to New Bedford). The boats would arrive from New Bedford and dock under the cliffs. People from Aquinnah would gather, the men cutting blocks of clay, and the women forming a chain to pass the clay onto the boats.

The cliffs have always provided for Wampanoags through fishing, clay, and tourism. Today, the cliffs are a majestic, historical monument that offer tribal members revenue through tourism. The cliffs also offer a watchful place and became the home of the Gay Head Light and Coast Guard Station. In 1966, the US Government declared the cliff area a Registered National Landmark.

Moshup and Pottap
The Whale

By catching whales as they came near to shore, Moshup became the first whaler in Aquinnah. He would take the whale to his den, often inviting other community members to eat with him. He'd keep great fires going, to cook the whale; and, to feed the fires, he'd pull up the trees. That's why today they say there is a scarcity of trees in Aquinnah. Moshup would also direct Wampanoags to schools of black fish and help them sight whales; it is fitting that many of his children and followers took up whaling.

Like Moshup, the Wampanoags started whaling right from the beach. The two kinds of whales they hunted were the black fish, or grampuses, and the right whale. Whales would swim near the shore to feed and the Wampanoags would hunt them from dug-out canoes. Soon, however, beach whaling gave way to deep sea whaling and Wampanoags were recruited because of their familiarity with the habits of whales. By the 1880s, whaling was a sure path to money, exposure to the outside world, pride, and adventure. Whaling served as a means for Aquinnah Wampanoags to leave the Island for economic gain—literally going around the world in whaling ships.

Amos Smalley (1877-1961)

The most famous of the Wampanoag whalers is my Uncle Amos Smalley, the harpooner who brought in the White Whale—believed to be Melville's Moby Dick. Amos was born in Aquinnah in 1877. As a young boy, Uncle Amos had heard stories of Moshup—the real pioneer of whaling. At fifteen, Amos went to sea on a New Bedford whaler. He spent four years on Pearl Nelson. Then, two years later, he sailed out on the Bark Platina. It was on the Platina, in July of 1902, south of the Azores, that he harpooned the 90 foot-long great white whale. This rare, and fear-inspiring being, was believed to be over 100 years old and ran more than 80 barrels of oil.

Amos and Addie Smalley

On his return to Aquinnah, Uncle Amos told us that when he saw the Great White Whale he remembered the story of the last great Sachem of Aquinnah—Mittark. On his death bed, Mittark warned of strangers coming to Aquinnah. As a sign of his prophecy, he said a great white whale would rise out of Witch Pond. Uncle Amos also remembered that when Moshup took leave of Aquinnah, he constructed a secret tunnel from the cliffs to Witch Pond so his pet white whale could seek safety and refuge. Why, even today, when we see fog over Witch Pond or feel the fog's moisture on our face, we say the White Whale is spouting her plume.

Legend of Moshup's Bridge

My grandmother told me that there would be no lighthouse or roads in Aquinnah without the legends of Moshup's Bridge—a dangerous reef off the Aquinnah Cliffs. Moshup's Bridge, which the English insisted on calling Devil's Bridge, is a square mile of submerged rocks—part of the continental shelf. It is the site of a number of shipwrecks, including the famed City of Columbus. The City of Columbus was sailing on January 18, 1884, from Boston to Savannah, Georgia, when it struck Moshup's Bridge. The boat that went to the rescue in the midst of a blizzard was manned by "Gay Headers"—showing our bravery and compassion. Thanks to their heroic efforts, 29 of the 132 people on board were rescued from the frigid waters.

Three Versions of the Legend

The first version of the legend states that Moshup wished to go to the neighboring island of Cuttyhunk with dry feet, so he started to build a bridge of stones. Unfortunately, before he could finish, a large crab bit his big toe. Moshup dropped his stones and threw the crab out to sea, forming Noman's Island. Moshup went home, the bridge unfinished.

A second version is that Gay Head's opinion was divided as to whether there should be a bridge to Cuttyhunk where Gosnold, the English explorer (who renamed Noepe Martha's Vineyard) had set up a settlement to harvest sassafras. Cheepie, a mischievous spirit, agreed to build the bridge if his work could be completed between sunset and the first crow of the rooster. Around midnight, an old woman of the anti-bridge group flashed a lit candle in the eyes of her rooster. The rooster crowed and Cheepie, thinking it was morning, left the bridge unfinished.

The third version is that Moshup, to keep up his fires, pulled up the largest trees by the roots and, to satisfy his hunger, cooked fish of the sea. To facilitate catching fish, he threw many large stones into the sea on which he might walk with greater ease. Now, this is called Moshup's Bridge.

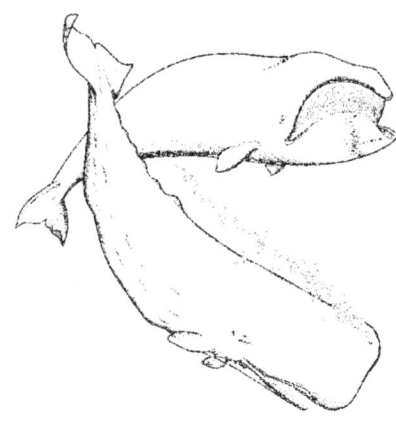

AQUINNAH MEMORIES

Lighthouse

The first lighthouse came to Aquinnah in 1799. Forty feet tall and sitting up on the head of the cliffs, it was made of wood and the light was produced by fourteen sperm whale oil-burning lamps. By 1850, the lighthouse keeper demanded a road be built to facilitate the arrival of supplies. Six years later, the current 60 foot brick lighthouse and keeper's cottage was erected and the old sperm oil lit lens was replaced by a Fresnel lens. The Fresnel lens had been exhibited at the World's Fair in London. It was eight feet high and four feet in diameter, weighed four and a half tons and was arranged in a system of 1,003 glass prisms. The light was visible for over 20 miles at sea. In 1952, a high-intensity electric beacon replaced the Fresnel lens. The lens was reinstalled on the grounds of the Dukes County Historical Society where it still can be seen today. Shortly after, in 1956, the keeper's dwelling was torn down and the light became fully automatic.

The Aquinnah Light

Tourism

Prior to 1850 there were no roads in Aquinnah. Because of this, most of the travel and trade was with New Bedford via boat. The remoteness was highlighted in tourism books and people came to see the rare scenery and the cliffs, to search for fossils, and to see the famous Fresnel Lens. At the end of the 19th Century, a popular excursion was to take a steamer from New Bedford, Providence or Edgartown to Aquinnah's Steamboat Landing, on what is now Lighthouse Road; the fare was 50 cents. Five steamers made regular excursions to Aquinnah every Sunday.

Excursion Flyer 1886

By the late nineteenth century, numerous residents in town were involved in tourism, providing overnight lodging, food, oxcart rides and selling articles made from the clay. People would leave their orders at the nearby restaurants and stop to dine on their return. Typical menus included clam or fish chowder, baked fish with stuffing, potatoes and cream sauces over fish, hot rolls, lobster, apple or blueberry pie—all for another 50 cents. At the dock there was a pavilion where dances were held, a restaurant, and an inn. There were many inns, including Edwin DeVries Vanderhoop's nineteen-room hotel. Later on, there were many restaurants—the Totem Pole, the Wigwam, the Potters Wheel, Thunderbird, Sugar and Spice, The North Shore Inn, The Broken Arrow, the Not-A-Way, and the Vanderhoop Restaurant. Sometime later, there was Mannings. After World War I, the car replaced the steamship for transporting tourists. The roads were better and people started just coming for the day. Today, restaurants remain open along with the shops at the cliffs; but the pier, the hotels and pavilion are gone.

Excursionist at Pilot Landing 1888

Aquinnah boat and crew that saved wrecked City of Columbus, January 14, 1782

Recipes from the Collection of Helen Manning

Cranberry Crisp

Mix together cup of brown sugar, cup of flour, a pinch of cinnamon, and four cups of whole fresh cranberries. Toss well and put in a well-greased pie pan or baking dish. Top the fruit with a blended mixture of one cup brown sugar, cup flour, cup oats, and a stick of butter cut in pieces. Bake at 375 till top is brown and fruit bubbles - around 35 minutes. Cranberry Crisp is always a desert favorite at the Fall Social following Cranberry Days.

Plum Porridge Recipe From Hattie Cooper

Plum Porridge is a special Aquinnah dish. First, parboil raisins and pour off the water. Add fresh water and boil until tender. Heat a quart of milk and add sugar to taste, also butter and nutmeg. Bring slowly to a boil, taking care not to scorch the milk. Add a bit of oat flour for thickening. At the end, add raisins.

Potato Bargain

In an iron frying pan with lid, fry cubed cut-up salt pork until crisp. Remove the salt pork and add 3 onions sliced thin. Sauté the onions until golden and put back the salt pork and 5 potatoes that you have sliced thin. (Hint: parboil the potatoes.) Add boiling water to cover the potatoes and onions, add salt and pepper and cover tightly. Cook over a low flame. Turn the potatoes every so often. When potatoes are soft and the water boils out, then turn off the heat.

After a long winter when supplies were low and scallop season had not yet begun, we ate what my mother called Potato Bargain. Salt pork is still used to add flavor to dishes - before it was used because it kept well and was less expensive than butter.

Herring Roe Recipe

Remove roe from herring. Roll in mixture of flour and corn meal. Now fry in butter or bake with bacon strips.

Quahog Chowder

The hard shell clam, or quahog, is the clam of choice for chowder in Aquinnah. One can go out and dig up a bushel of quahogs, but now many folks just go and buy a quart of shucked quahogs for their chowder. Take the quahogs out of their clam juice and chop them coarsely. I usually put the clam juice through cheesecloth to remove any sand, although the quahog ingest less sand than the steamer clam. In a heavy pot cook 1/3 cup diced salt port until crisp. Remove. Add 3-4 finely chopped onions (optional) to the fat in the pot, cooking until soft and golden. Add about 4 cups diced potatoes, the clam liquid which you have strained and water to cover over the potatoes. Simmer until potatoes are tender but not overcooked. Add the chopped clams and the salt pork. In another pan, heat a quart of light cream or half and half along with 4 tablespoons of butter - do not boil. Add to the chowder. Add salt and pepper - taste first. The salt pork adds its own flavor. Remove from heat and allow to sit to collect its flavor. Remember do not boil or your chowder will curdle.

Beach Plum Jelly

The beach plum is a native American shrub. Wash plums, pick over, cover with water, bring to a boil, drain, and discard water. Return plums to the pot, add boiling water to cover, and cook until the fruit is soft, mashing them once or twice. Turn the fruit and juice into a jelly bag, made of several thickness of cheesecloth, hanging over a large bowl. Allow it to drain until no more juice drips through. Some people let it drain all night. For clear jelly do not squeeze the bag or the jelly will be cloudy. Add 1 cup sugar to each cup juice, boil to jelly stage (usually 5 minutes), skim and pour into sterile jelly jars. Seal with two layers of melted paraffin and the lids. Store in a cool dark place. Some cooks like to simply follow directions on the pectin box.

Cranberry Day and Cranberries

Moshup's wife, Squant, was the caretaker of the cranberry bogs and convened the first cranberry day. The cranberry is one of the few fruits native to North America; others include grapes and blueberries. It is widely held that the wild cranberry, or *sassamanesh* in Wampanoag, is rich in Vitamin C and has medicinal and nutritional properties. Tamson Weeks, a Wampanoag herbalist, used cranberries to heal a variety of complaints including blood disorders, stomach aliments, liver problems, scurvy and fever. She also said a poultice of cranberries could cure cancer.

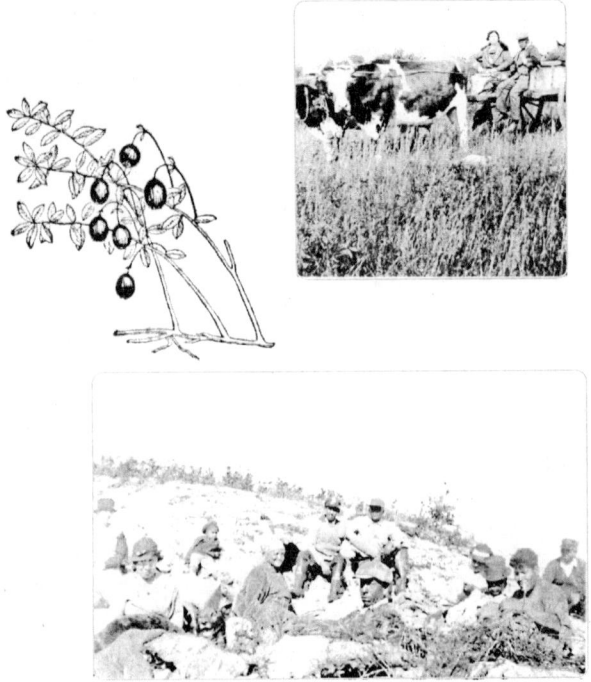

Cranberry Day Celebration

Cranberry day marked the end of the summer season and the time for families to move inland to winter camps and away from the winds of the sea. For over a century Cranberry day has been the second Tuesday in October; and, as recent as the 1930s, it was a time to prepare for winter. Prior to the 1938 hurricane, the harvest was sold in New Bedford and the proceeds used to purchase the winter staples of molasses, sugar and flour. Extra money helped the elderly and the poor. The bogs were an important part of the economy, with harvesting taking up to three days. People would pitch tents, cook quahog chowder over fires and at night a bonfire would be lit. Then people would tell stories, and there would be dancing to fiddle music.

"All the natives of Gay Head would travel in their ox-carts, carrying a lunch time feast of baked chicken, pies and all the fixings. At noon everyone would spread their lunches out in the bogs and different families would invite others to share their meal. The people would begin harvesting at dawn; originally, most of the harvesting was by hand. The cranberry scoop, as we know it, was not yet used. Some harvesting was done using a long handled box with metal teeth which was raked through the vines so you would not have to get down on your hands and knees."

—*Leonard Vanderhoop's Cranberry Report*

Wampum

Moshup and Squant used to select shells for adornment. Many times, they selected the beautiful purple and white shell of the quahog clam. The tubular, purple and white shell beads, known as wampum, were woven into belts and headdresses. Moshup and Squant taught that wampum is sacred and, since we did not have a written language, could be used as a permanent record of an event such as an agreement or alliance with other Native Peoples. Wampum, to the Eastern Algonquin, was a way of communicating peace and commitment. Explorers and the English misunderstood the exchange of wampum to have a monetary purpose, but this was not true. In the early seventeenth century, only the Sachems were able to wear wampum as adornment. Today, it is worn by Wampanoags and non-Wampanoags. When one wears wampum today, it is important to remember its significance. I am happy to say that in the past few years a number of Wampanoag people have reclaimed the skill of working with wampum and are teaching it to the children.

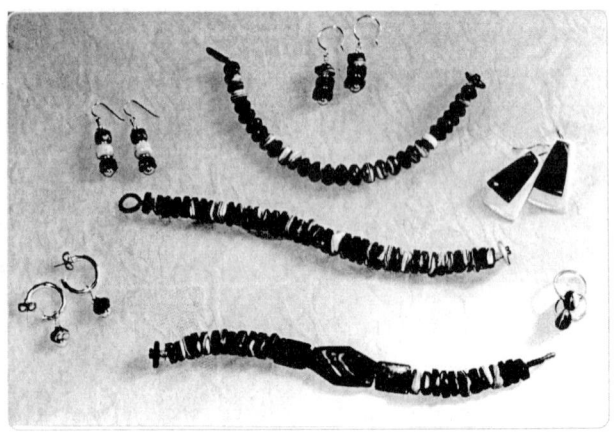

Modern Wampum Jewelry

Herring

The herring creek in Aquinnah is a natural run that still runs today. Herring "run", or come in from the salt water, to fresh water each spring, to return to where they were spawned. In the old days, families would gather at the herring run and camp until the end of the run. Herring was used as fertilizer for the corn. As for the fresh herring, we only took what could last a week, then smoked or salted the rest for winter. Someone discovered that the scales from the herring were luminescent and started making jewelry from the scales, known as priscilla pearls. Today, when the shade trees blossom and the osprey return, the herring start to run.

Scalloping

Today, the tribe is preparing a shellfish hatchery at the Herring Creek. The shellfish in the ponds, according to archeologists, are the same as those our ancestors collected thousands of years ago. The Wampanoags have been scalloping in Aquinnah since 2270 BC. Scalloping was traditionally done by the men; but, in the 1950s, women demanded their right to scallop and received their scalloping license. Today, scalloping season runs from October into April and a town resident can get a commercial or a family permit. Whole families set out for scalloping, as long as the temperature is above freezing, so the scallops do not die before getting to market. The scallops from the ponds in Aquinnah are the sweetest in the world and the $19 per pound selling price at the market attest to that.

Language

The Wopanaak, or Massachusett, language is an Eastern Algonguin language, similar to Natick, Narragansett, Mohegan-Pequot, Montauk and Ouiripi-Unquachoag. The language territory covers the coastal region of the Merrimac River, south Narragansett Bay, and Cape Cod. Before the arrival of the English, a written Wampanoag language did not exist. The language was spoken and passed on, generation to generation. Today, using historical documentation of the written language produced in the 1600s by missionaries and native speakers, and with the assistance of linguists and language classes initiated and created by Wampanoags, the people of Aquinnah and Mashpee are reclaiming our language. With the help of linguistic experts, a short and long term plan is being developed to see this ambitious project through to fruition. The Wampanaog Language Reclamation Project is much to credit for this great reclamation of this important aspect of our culture.

And the Wampanoags of Aquinnah Today?

Today, we are a federally recognized tribe—the Wampanoag Tribe of Gay Head/Aquinnah—meaning we are a sovereign nation with a nation to nation relationship with the United States of America. The US Government recognizes that we had maintained and governed ourselves long before the United States of America was formed. Membership is 900 plus, and we have a wonderful tribal multipurpose building—constructed with our culture and the environment in mind. Like Moshup and the Sachems, we have a Council form of Government. We have self-government in the areas of Health, Economic Development, Education, Human Services, Natural Resources, Finance, and Aid to Tribal Government.

We are in the process of reclaiming our language; and, we have brought back the drum. Every summer we honor and re-enact the story of Moshup's life, weaving together narration, drumming and dance in the Pageant of Moshup.

We offer cultural programs to tribal members and their families so they can learn more about pottery, wampum and basketry. We have a Spring and Harvest Social. We still celebrate Cranberry Day every second Tuesday in October; and, we are repatriating our ancestors' remains and belongings from museums and known grave sites. We are building a shellfish hatchery and the Aquinnah Cultural Center—a living history museum.

Although some of our former industries, like the Gay Head Clay Co, the cranberry bogs, and the manufacturing of priscilla pearls have ended, we continue the tradition of fishing, scalloping, the herring run, tourism, and making jewelry—wampum—from the shell of the quahog clam. Some elders still make pottery and jewelry from the clay on the cliffs and pass this skill on to our youths.

We know that Moshup is still here because we live the lessons he taught our ancestors in the first school on the Aquinnah Cliffs. We still honor sacred sites, especially the colorful clay cliffs, home of Moshup. We help each other, like Moshup helped us, caretaking our elders and children. Although, like everyone, we eat a variety of foods, we still have our traditional foods: fish, venison, corn, scallops, herring, cranberries, rosehips, beach plums, squash and beans. And, like Moshup and the Sachems, we continue our council form of government and observe the ceremonial cycle, keeping cranberry day a holiday and continuing our spring and harvest socials.

And Moshup?

From our legends we know that Moshup began having dreams of visits by a strange people from a far off land. He dreamed they would be pale-skinned and speak a new tongue. They would come one day to Aquinnah to live. Moshup knew his dreams were a warning and he knew his children would never lift a hand against a neighbor, so he called a family council. He told his family that soon there would not be room on Aquinnah for him and Squant. He began to prepare to take leave. He told his children that in order to find refuge from harm, those who wished could be turned into killer whales, free to roam the sea.

Moshup's toad turned to stone on Moshup's leaving

Others of his children went to Takemmy and Nunnepog and settled in the Sachemships there with their cousins. So, he went to visit them and reminded them to never forget their way of life. To protect his pet toad, who was larger than a person, he turned him into stone. For many years after, before there was such a thing as a post office, people would leave messages for each other at Toad Rock. Children are still brought to see Toad Rock to remind them that Moshup truly lived here.

Moshup gazed sorrowfully for the last time upon the home which he had created, the place where he had lived so happily and ruled so wisely for many years. Together,

Moshup and Squant started their final journey along the cliffs, without a single glance back. They passed Peaked Rock and Black Brook; their footsteps ended near Zack's Cliffs.

Today, when the atmosphere is clear, we look in that direction and see the fog creeping up along the dunes. We say, "Moshup has dumped his *peeudlee* (pipe)." We know that the smoke stands as a sign of his love for us. Yes Aquinnah, Moshup still lives here.

Wohkuhquishik — The End

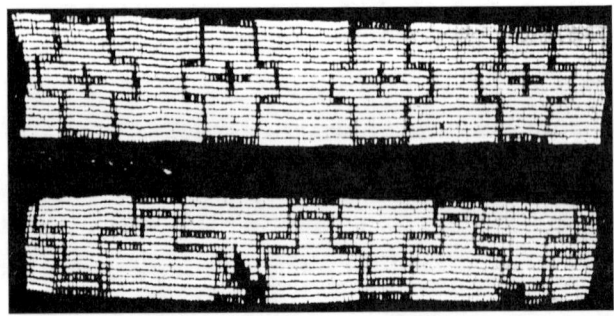

Historical Time Line

This time line is to provide the reader with a brief understanding of the history of Noepe and the Wampanoag Nation of Gay Head/Aquinnah. For more information, see the source list at the end of this booklet.

12,500-10,000 BC
First evidence of Wampanoag and other Eastern Algonquin Nation settlements used for hunting and fishing, not permanent residences. Archeological evidence at Squibnocket Pond and Lucy Vincent Beach have confirmed this.

3,000 BC
Moshup, the giant father of the Wampanoag people, arrives with his family and creates the Island of Noepe, land of bitter waters, now known as Martha's Vineyard.

2270 BC
Eastern Algonquin and Wampanoag hunters of the inland forest of New England come to Aquinnah.

2190 BC
Eastern Algonquin and Wampanoag people come to harvest shellfish. Hunters are now using arrows with quartz tip heads.

1380 AD
Ancestors of the Aquinnah Wampanoags establish permanent settlements on Noepe. They use mortar and pestles, shell tempered clay pots and bake in earthen ovens.

1602 AD
First recorded contact with English. Gosnold renames Noepe (land amidst the waters) Martha's Vineyard and renames Aquinnah (land beneath the hill) Gay Head after the gaily colored clay cliffs

1611 AD
Wampanoag Sachem, Epenow, is captured and sold as a slave in Europe. Epenow convinces his English owner of gold on Martha's Vineyard and returns as a guide.

Epenow arranges a carefully planned escaped where the English captain is wounded and later dies.

1620 AD
Pilgrims arrive in Plymouth. Epenow's fame evokes fear and Pilgrims do not venture to the offshore islands

1633 AD
Law of Massachusetts Bay Colony confirms Indian title to all lands on Noepe.

1641 AD
Deed granting "Martha's Vineyard" to Thomas Mayhew Sr. is given by the King of England.

1643 AD
Thomas Mayhew Jr. arrives before his father and establishes English Settlement with a small number of white settlers (20 families) in Edgartown. Three thousand Wampanoags are living on the Island. Thomas Mayhew Jr. converts the first Wampanoag, Hiacoomes, to Christianity.

1645 AD
Universal sickness, or plague, affects Wampanoag population. Using medicine, the English try to prove their God is more benevolent and powerful than the Wampanoag Creator. The goal of the English is pacification through Christianity. As Sachems convert and sell land to the English, the inhabitants of the sachemdom are displaced. People have little choice but to convert since civil control and censure is administered through the Congregational Church. The Wampanoag people who resist conversion are pushed up-island.

1657 AD
Thomas Mayhew Jr. sets off to England from Boston. His ship never arrives and his father, Thomas Sr., continues his work of conversion. By the time of Thomas Mayhew Jr.'s death, he has converted over ten percent of the population. He creates Christian Indiantowns similar to the English settlements but subordinate to them.

1663 AD
Mayhew Sr. converts the Wampanoag Sachem of Aquinnah, Mittark. Aquinnah has been the most resistant to conversion and Mittark is banished. After three years, he is forgiven and is allowed to return to Aquinnah where he is preacher and Sachem.

1663 AD
First Wampanoag graduates from Harvard University.

1674 AD
In 30 years, the tribal population is reduced by half by influenza brought by the English; 1500 Wampanoags remain.

1675 AD
Indian title to Gay Head confirmed by deed.

1675-1677
King Philip Indian Wars.

1683 AD
Mittark, the Sachem, dies.

1687 AD
Matthew Mayhew (Thomas Mayhew Sr.'s grandson) moves to extinguish Indian title to land at "Gay Head". He accompanies Joseph Mittark, who had succeeded his father as Sachem, to New York where Joseph Mittark sells the land. The sale is challenged by members of the tribe, who pointed to prohibition against such an action, by Mittark, before his death.

1694 AD
Aquinnah Wampanoags rebel by rejecting Congregational Church and establishing the Gay Head Baptist Church.

1711 AD
The London-based Company of Propagation of the Gospel purchases Gay Head, ostensibly in order to protect and isolate the Tribe. The Company digs a two foot deep and four foot wide trench across the land which joins Gay Head and Chilmark and plants thorny shrubs and erects a gate.

1720 AD

By the early eighteenth century, there are only 800 Wampanoags in 155 families.

1727 AD

The Company agrees to deed back to the tribe all but 800 acres of land. The tribe receives an important legal basis for occupation on their land when ten members of the tribe agree to release 800 acres of land in exchange for the Company's deed granting the rest of the land to the tribe.

1776 AD

Following the American revolution, The Propagation of the Gospel return to England leaving the land to the tribe. The tribe farms and holds lands in common.

1790 AD

The Non-Intercourse Act prohibits extinguishment of Indian title without Federal approval.

1799 AD

Gay Head light is built. Massachusetts, recognizing the autonomy of the Wampanoags, obtains a conveyance of a small tract of land for construction of the lighthouse.

1807 AD

A traveler writes in his diary of Gay Head that there are no trees or roads in Gay Head. He documents 26 houses framed, 7 wetus, 3 barns and 2 meeting houses. He is told that over 100 people are gone from the community—either children put in the service of English families in Chilmark and Edgartown, or men who have left to go whaling. To earn a living, they sell cranberries and clay and lease lands to whites.

1814 AD

Commonwealth of Massachusetts attempts to control Wampanoags at Gay Head by enacting "guardians" to seize lands for unpaid rent. Wampanoags refuse to accept authority of the guardians and continue to hold land in common.

1827

Gay Head School is built. There still are no roads and travel is by catboats and trade is with merchants in New Bedford.

1840 AD

The State of Massachusetts puts in a road (now known as State Road) for the convenience of the light house keeper. New road results in the movement of the town center from Old South Road to the more traveled State Road.

1850s AD

Tourism begins. Steamers from New Bedford bring tourists who enjoy oxcart rides from Pilot Landing to the "Gay Head" light and the cliffs.

1854 AD

Wampanaogs are part of the Underground Railroad

1857 AD

Gay Head School expands.

1862 AD

Massachusetts starts to assert control over the Wampanoags by declaring "district status".

1870 AD

"Gay Head" becomes an incorporated town. The Wampanoag's "accepted" town status but had opposed the incorporation . All common lands, funds and rights held by the Indian district are transferred to the Town of "Gay Head". According to oral history of Winona Silva: "How clearly the people saw that they did not want to become a town -they circulated a petition throughout the town saying they wanted to stay in Massachusetts, but as an Indian district -they were afraid of losing territory -they weren't interested in private property- they were interested in sharing their lands Massachusetts -established the town -divided the land-then time from time when people could not pay taxes -other people would come in -pay the tax- take the land-they'd say if you want your land back-pay me back but that never happened."

1871 AD
First Census reports 55 families and a total of 227 people.

1880 AD
Ballot box voting comes to Gay Head.

1888 AD
Edwin DeVries Vanderhoop is first Wampanoag to become a State Representative to the Massachusetts General Court representing Dukes County.

1917 AD
Aquinnah furnishes to the United States Armed Forces the largest number of men in proportion to population of any town in New England to fight in World War I.

1932 AD
Wampanoag tribe reenacts powwow pageant of Moshup over a three day period on the cliffs.

1951 AD
Electricity comes to Gay Head for the first time. (The other island towns had received electricity prior to WWII.)

1958 AD
Moshup Trail is completed.

1966 AD
U.S. Department of Interior lists Aquinnah Cliffs as a National Landmark.

1968 AD
Gay Head one-room school house is closed. Five children in four grades transferred to West Tisbury School. First woman elected to Gay Head Board of Selectmen. First of only two women ever elected to GHBS. Both women are Wampanoag—Thelma Weisberg and Helen Manning (author).

1972 AD
Wampanoag Tribal Council of Gay Head Aquinnah Incorporated (WTCGHA) is formed to promote self determination, to ensure preservation and continuation

of Wampanoag history and culture, to achieve Federal Recognition for the Tribe and to seek to return Tribal Land to the Wampanoag people.

1974 AD

Tribal Council files suit in Federal District Court for the return of the Tribal Common Lands in the Town of Gay Head. Tribal Council claims that the 1870 Act that terminated the Indian title and transferred Common Lands to the Town was in violation of the 1790 Non-Intercourse Law.

1983 AD

Tribe submits petition for federal recognition.

1983 AD

Indian Claim Settlement is signed. State will convey 238 acres of public land to the Tribe (the Common Lands) and the Federal Government will finance the purchase of 180 acres.

1987 AD

Wampanoag Tribe of Gay Head Aquinnah receives federal recognition from the Bureau of Indian Affairs granting the Wampanoag Nation nation-to-nation status with the US Federal Government. Indian Claim Settlement Act is signed in Congress authorizing the appropriation of $2.2 million of Federal monies to the tribe to finance the purchase of land.

1994 AD

Tribal multipurpose building completed that hosts various offices and provides for Council meetings, tribal socials and general membership meetings.

1996 AD

Affordable tribal housing is completed, allowing members of the tribe to follow their dream to return to Aquinnah.

1998 AD

Scalloping returns to Aquinnah after a 13 year hiatus.

1998 AD

Aquinnah Cultural Center forms Board of Directors and

becomes a nonprofit organization. The goal of the ACC is to open a living museum and provide for cultural enrichment through classes and programs for all tribal members.

1999 AD
Aquinnah Cultural Center produces the Wampanoag Way: Aquinnah Cultural Trail Map.

Bibliographic Sources
Joan Lester, *We're still Here-the Art of New England*, The Children's Museum Collection, 1987, Children's Museum, Boston, MA.

William Ritchie, *The Archaelology of Martha's Vineyard*, The Natural History Press, Garden City, NY, 1969.

William Simmons, *The Spirit of New England Tribes-Indian History and Folklore*, University Press of New England, Hanover, 1986

Monographs and Articles
Edward, Burgess., "The Old South Road of Gay Head 1926, Dukes County Intelligencer, Vol. 12, No.1, 1970
Helen Attaquin, A Brief History of Gay Head
Dorothy Scovel, Indian Legends of Martha's Vineyard
Arthur Railton, The English and the Indians on Martha's Vineyard, Duke County Intelligencer. Part I-IV, Vol 31 No.4; Vol. 32 No.2; Vol. 33 No.1, Vol. 33 No.3; and Vol. 34 No.3; May, 1990-February, 1993.
Wampanoag Way: An Aquinnah Cultural Tour. The Aquinnah Cultural Center, Aquinnah, MA. 1999
Oral Histories and Conversations with Tribal Elders:
  Helen Vanderhoop Manning
  Winona Silva
  Maysel Vanderhoop
  Alfred Vanderhoop

Photo Credits
Tourism and lighthouse photographs from Martha's Vineyard Historical Society Archives (pp. 34-37); wampum (p. 42) Derrill Bazzy; Helen Manning at light (p.12) Betsy Corsiglia. All others from the collection of Helen Manning.